Dachshunds

Susan H. Gray
and
Warren Rylands

www.av2books.com

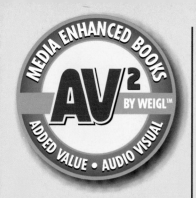

AV² provides enriched content that supplements and complements this book. Weigl's AV² books strive to create inspired learning and engage young minds in a total learning experience.

Your AV² Media Enhanced books come alive with...

Audio
Listen to sections of the book read aloud.

Key Words
Study vocabulary, and complete a matching word activity.

Go to www.av2books.com, and enter this book's unique code.

Video
Watch informative video clips.

Quizzes
Test your knowledge.

BOOK CODE

X 8 6 4 2 8 2

Embedded Weblinks
Gain additional information for research.

Slide Show
View images and captions, and prepare a presentation.

AV² by Weigl brings you media enhanced books that support active learning.

Try This!
Complete activities and hands-on experiments.

... and much, much more!

Published by AV² by Weigl
350 5th Avenue, 59th Floor
New York, NY 10118
Website: www.av2books.com

Library of Congress Cataloging-in-Publication Data

Names: Gray, Susan Heinrichs, author | and Rylands, Warren, author.
Title: Dachshunds / Susan H. Gray and Warren Rylands.
Description: New York, NY : AV2 by Weigl, [2017] | Series: All about dogs |
  Includes bibliographical references and index.
Identifiers: LCCN 2016004427 (print) | LCCN 2016007004 (ebook) | ISBN
  9781489645890 (hard cover : alk. paper) | ISBN 9781489650177 (soft cover :
  alk. paper) | ISBN 9781489645906 (Multi-user ebk.)
Subjects: LCSH: Dachshunds--Juvenile literature.
Classification: LCC SF429.D25 G682 2017 (print) | LCC SF429.D25 (ebook) | DDC
  636.753/8--dc23
LC record available at http://lccn.loc.gov/2016004427

Printed in the United States of America in Brainerd, Minnesota
1 2 3 4 5 6 7 8 9 0 20 19 18 17 16

072016
071416

Project Coordinator: Warren Rylands   Art Director: Terry Paulhus

Dachshunds

Contents

Name That Dog

What little dog has a big, loud voice?

What dog pouts when it is corrected?

What dog can squeeze through underground tunnels?

What dog can earn thousands of dollars at work?

Did you say the dachshund (DOKS-hundt)?

Then you are correct !

The Badger-Dog

Years ago, people in Europe hunted badgers. These big, furry animals live underground. Hunters often used dogs to track the badgers. The best dogs had short legs and long bodies. They could chase badgers right through their tunnels. The dogs' strong legs could dig through the dirt.

In the 1600s, people in Germany began calling these dogs "dachshunds." The word means "badger-dogs." Germans raised the dogs to hunt badgers and other animals.

The map to the right shows where Germany is on Earth. The map below shows a closer view.

Norway

Sweden

North Sea

Denmark

Esto

Great Britain

Lat

Lithuan

Neth.

Germany

Poland

Belgium

Lux.

Czech

France

Switzerland

Slovakia

Austria

Hungary

Slovenia

Croatia

Bosnia And Herz.

Italy

Yugoslavia

After a while, there were two sizes of dachshund. The bigger ones hunted badgers. They also hunted wild pigs called boars. The smaller ones chased foxes and hares. Both kinds of dachshunds had a great sense of smell. They could follow other animals' **scents**. They could track the animals through forests. They could track them across open fields. They could track them right down into their burrows.

In the 1800s, people brought little dachshunds to the United States. People loved them. Today, dachshunds are very **popular**. In fact, they are the sixth most popular dog **breed** in the United States.

People have all sorts of nicknames for dachshunds. They call them dachsies (DOK-seez), wiener dogs, and sausage dogs.

Dachshunds are the smallest breed of hunting dog.

Just Like Hot Dogs

Dachshunds have short legs and long bodies. Although they are small, they are very strong. They have deep chests. They have powerful legs for digging.

The dogs come in two sizes, standard and **miniature**. Most standard dachshunds weigh 16 to 32 pounds (7 to 15 kilograms). Many are 8 to 9 inches (20 to 23 centimeters) tall at the shoulder. Miniature dachshunds weigh only about 11 pounds (5 kg). They are often only 5 to 6 inches (13 to 15 cm) tall at the shoulder.

Some owners like to dress their wiener dogs in costumes. One outfit is simply a big foam hot-dog bun.

Dachshunds belong to a group of dogs called hounds. Hounds are excellent hunters. They have a good sense of smell. Basset hounds and beagles are hounds, too.

Dachshunds have three different kinds of coats. Smooth-haired dachsies have a short, thick coat. Long-haired dachsies have long, soft fur. It can be straight or a little wavy. Wire-haired dachshunds have hard, straight, wiry hairs. Dachshunds come in just about any color except white. They can be reddish, cream-colored, black, brown, or gray. Some are even spotted.

All dachshunds have long heads and floppy ears. They have dark eyes and smart-looking faces. Their eyebrows go up and down. Their faces seem to show lots of feelings.

Dachsies have lots of energy. They are smart, too. They are bold and sure of themselves.

Dachshunds with longer hair need more brushing than dachshunds with short hair.

A Mind of Its Own

Dachshunds are friendly, loving little dogs. They like to snuggle. They will even burrow under bed covers. They are **loyal** to their owners, too. Most dachsies get along with other pets.

Dachshunds make good pets for adults. They are fine for families with older children. Young children might hurt or trip over these little dogs. Dachshunds sometimes nip at small children, just to protect themselves.

Miniature dachshunds weigh up to 11 pounds (5 kg).

Some people may not like that dachshunds have a loud bark. It is important to learn about each dog breed before adoption.

Dachshunds have loud voices for such small dogs. Loud barking helps when the dogs go hunting. Owners always know where the dogs are, even when they are underground.

When dachshunds get mad, they stay mad. If you correct them, they pout until they get over it.

Dachshunds are not for everybody. They can be hard to train. They are certainly smart enough to learn tricks. However, they can be hard-headed and stubborn. They sometimes refuse to **obey** their owners.

Dachsies are loud barkers. They often bark at much larger dogs. They also bark at visitors and strangers. Sometimes, their loud barking is a good thing. These dogs make great watchdogs. They notice when something is wrong. Dachshunds have saved their owners from fires and other dangers.

Dachshund Puppies

Most dachshund mothers have three or four puppies in a **litter**. Sometimes, they have eight or nine. Each newborn is about as heavy as a lemon. The pups already have long bodies and short legs.

Adult dachshunds have long, narrow heads. Newborns have round heads. Their faces have wrinkles. Their eyes do not open for the first two weeks. The pups stay with their mother. They just want to eat, sleep, and keep warm.

Dachshund puppies can be hard to house train. They are smart, but also very stubborn. Training should start early.

It is easy to hurt a dachshund puppy's back. You should hold the pup carefully, with both hands. Be careful not to let its back sag.

Dachshund puppies eat a lot. At one year, a dachsie weighs 25 times its birth weight.

After about five weeks, the pups move around more. They wander away from their mother, but they do not stay away for long. They still like to be with their family.

As they get older, the pups get braver. They play and run around with their brothers and sisters. That is how they learn to get along with other dogs. They get interested in things around them, too. They go farther away from their mother. By the time they are eight weeks old, they are ready to be adopted. They are ready to join a new family.

Dachshund puppies love to play, but they should not be taken outside until they are six to eight weeks old.

Dachshunds Go To Work

Most people keep dachshunds just as pets. They can be wonderful pets. Sometimes they are even heroes. In Oregon, a dachshund named Peter warned his owners of a house fire. The owners got out safely. Peter got an award for his bravery.

Some owners enter their dachshunds in **contests**. In some contests, the dogs show that they are nice looking and well behaved. In others, they show how well they obey **commands**.

Dachshunds can be very good show dogs because they are so smart.

Dachshunds love to dig, even when they are not hunting for truffles. These dogs have been known to dig up flower beds in the backyard.

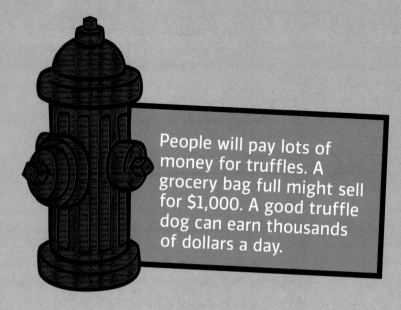

People will pay lots of money for truffles. A grocery bag full might sell for $1,000. A good truffle dog can earn thousands of dollars a day.

Some dachshunds work for a living instead. They hunt for rare plants called truffles. Truffles are sort of like mushrooms. They grow underground, on the roots of trees. They have a special smell. People love how they taste.

People once used pigs to find truffles. Now, they use dachshunds. Both pigs and dachshunds can smell truffles easily. Both animals also love to dig, but pigs do not stop digging. They find truffles and tear them up, or even eat them. Dachshunds are much easier to control. They do not eat the plants. They are the perfect truffle hunters.

Dachshunds are known for the way they run. Sometimes it looks like they are flying.

Caring for a Dachshund

Dachshunds make great pets, but they need special care. Their short legs and long backs hold up a lot of weight. These dogs should never jump down from chairs or sofas. Even a short jump can hurt them. They should not run up and down stairs. Sitting up and begging can hurt their backs, too.

Dachshunds do not need much exercise, but they do need some. Staying inside can make them lazy. They might eat too much and gain weight. Extra weight is hard on a dachshund's back.

There are special races for dachshunds. The Wiener Nationals are held in California every year. The dachshunds run along a short track. Thousands of people cheer them on.

When dachshunds go outdoors, they should stay on a leash. They love to chase other animals. If they see a squirrel or rabbit, they might take off. Then, they might get lost or hurt.

Dachshunds are easy to keep clean. The smooth-haired dogs are easiest. Owners can just wipe them down with a wet cloth. Long-haired and wire-haired dachsies need **grooming**. Brushing or combing keeps their coats clean and neat.

Healthy dachshunds live to be 14 or 15 years old. They make their owners very happy.

Dachshunds with short hair only need to be bathed every three to four months.

Dachshund Quiz

Q: What does "dachshund" mean?

A: Badger dogs

Q: The small dachshund breed is known for chasing which two animals?

A: Foxes and hares

Q: How long does it take for a newborn dachshund's eyes to open?

A: Two weeks

Q: How many puppies do most dachshund mothers have?

A: Three to four

Q: How big are dachshunds when they are born?

A: About the size of a lemon

Q: Dachshunds are great at hunting what kind of mushroom?

A: Truffles

Key Words

breed (BREED): a certain type of an animal

commands (kuh-MANDZ): orders to do certain things

contests (KON-tests): events where people or animals try to win by being the best

grooming (GROOM-ing): cleaning and brushing an animal

litter (LIH-tur): a group of babies born to one animal at the same time

loyal (LOY-ul): to be true to something and stand up for it

miniature (MIN-ee-uh-chur): small for its kind

obey (oh-BAY): to do what they are told

popular (PAH-pyuh-lur): liked by lots of people

scents (SENTS): the way something smells

Index

Log on to www.av2books.com

AV² by Weigl brings you media enhanced books that support active learning. Go to www.av2books.com, and enter the special code found on page 2 of this book. You will gain access to enriched and enhanced content that supplements and complements this book. Content includes video, audio, weblinks, quizzes, a slide show, and activities.

AV² Online Navigation

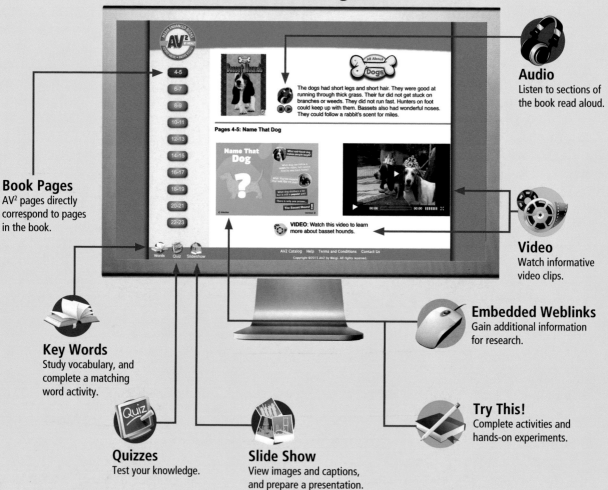

Book Pages
AV² pages directly correspond to pages in the book.

Key Words
Study vocabulary, and complete a matching word activity.

Quizzes
Test your knowledge.

Slide Show
View images and captions, and prepare a presentation.

Audio
Listen to sections of the book read aloud.

Video
Watch informative video clips.

Embedded Weblinks
Gain additional information for research.

Try This!
Complete activities and hands-on experiments.

AV² was built to bridge the gap between print and digital. We encourage you to tell us what you like and what you want to see in the future.

Sign up to be an AV² Ambassador at www.av2books.com/ambassador.